JELLYFISH
ARE BRAINLESS!

By Amanda Vink

Gareth Stevens
PUBLISHING

Please visit our website, www.garethstevens.com. For a free color catalog of all our high-quality books, call toll free 1-800-542-2595 or fax 1-877-542-2596.

Cataloging-in-Publication Data

Library of Congress Cataloging-in-Publication Data

Names: Vink, Amanda, author.
Title: Jellyfish are brainless! / Amanda Vink.
Description: New York : Gareth Stevens Publishing, [2020] | Series: Animals without brains! | Includes index.
Identifiers: LCCN 2019014923| ISBN 9781538245828 (paperback) | ISBN 9781538245842 (library bound) | ISBN 9781538245835 (6 pack)
Subjects: LCSH: Jellyfishes–Juvenile literature.
Classification: LCC QL377.S4 V56 2020 | DDC 593.5/3–dc23
LC record available at https://lccn.loc.gov/2019014923

Published in 2020 by
Gareth Stevens Publishing
111 East 14th Street, Suite 349
New York, NY 10003

Designer: Sarah Liddell
Editor: Amanda Vink

Photo credits: Cover, pp. 1, 15 Damsea/Shutterstock.com; background used throughout Sanjatosic/Shutterstock.com; p. 5 patrick vaccalluzzo/Shutterstock.com; p. 7 Martin Prochazkacz/Shutterstock.com; p. 9 Agarianna76/Shutterstock.com; p. 11 KT photo/Shutterstock.com; p. 13 Rebecca Schreiner/Shutterstock.com; p. 17 Happy Owl/Shutterstock.com; p. 19 David Rose/Shutterstock.com; p. 21 Ethan Daniels/Shutterstock.com.

Printed in the United States of America

Some of the images in this book illustrate individuals who are models. The depictions do not imply actual situations or events.

CPSIA compliance information: Batch #CW20GS: For further information contact Gareth Stevens, New York, New York at 1-800-542-2595.

CONTENTS

Brainless!. 4
An Invertebrate 6
Nerve Net .8
Hunt and Be Hunted 10
At Home Around the World. 12
Life Cycle of a Jellyfish 14
Polyps 16
Watch Out! 18
A Pool of Knowledge. 20
Glossary. .22
For More Information. 23
Index 24

Boldface words appear in the glossary.

Brainless!

Jellyfish are unusual and interesting creatures without brains! They aren't fish. They're **plankton**. Jellyfish are made of about 98 percent water, and they have **transparent** bodies. Jellyfish come in different colors. Some of them even glow in the dark!

An Invertebrate

Besides not having a brain, jellyfish also don't have a backbone or bony **skeleton**. This makes them part of the invertebrates, the largest group in the **animal kingdom**. Jellyfish have simple nervous systems, which control the body and help them respond to the world around them.

Nerve Net

Because a jellyfish doesn't have a brain, it needs another way to take in its world. A nerve net runs through its body. When **stimulated** by light or touch, the nerves tell the jellyfish to move.

Hunt and Be Hunted

Jellyfish are **carnivores**. Jellyfish eat **algae**, tiny plankton, and other ocean animals. Jellyfish move towards light and search for food using their tentacles, or long, bendable arms. Jellyfish are also eaten by many animals, including humans.

At Home Around the World

Jellyfish are found in oceans all around the world, in both warm water and cold water. Usually they are seen in salt water. Jellyfish have been around since before the dinosaurs. They're one of the oldest species, or kinds, of animal on Earth!

13

Life Cycle of a Jellyfish

An adult jellyfish is called a medusa. Jellyfish have a bell-shaped body, usually four fuzzy arms around their mouth and tentacles. They have a mouth at the center of their bodies, where they eat food and get rid of waste.

Polyps

An adult jellyfish drops eggs in the water. Those eggs turn into larvae and hook to the bottom of the ocean. They grow into polyps, which can **clone** themselves. Eventually they become ephyra, or a young jellyfish, and grow into adult jellyfish.

Watch Out!

A jellyfish tentacle can sting! A jellyfish stings both to keep itself safe and hunt. When a jellyfish touches another animal, stinging cells all over its tentacles reach out like poisonous darts. Some jellyfish are more dangerous to humans than others.

A Pool of Knowledge

Earth's air and oceans are getting warmer. Scientists think this may be causing the numbers of jellyfish to grow too large. While jellyfish are an important part of their **ecosystem**, too many can be harmful!

GLOSSARY

algae: plantlike living things that are mostly found in water

animal kingdom: a grouping that includes all living animals and animals that have died out

carnivore: an animal that eats meat

clone: a living thing that is an exact copy of another living thing

ecosystem: all the living things in an area

plankton: a tiny plant or animal that floats in the ocean

skeleton: the structure of bones that supports the body of a person or animal

stimulate: to make active or more active

transparent: letting light shine through

FOR MORE INFORMATION

BOOKS

Gish, Melissa. *Jellyfish*. Mankato, Minnesota: The Creative Company, 2016.

Rake, Jody S. *Jellyfish*. Mankato, Minnesota: Capstone Publishing, 2016.

WEBSITES

Jellyfish Facts!
www.natgeokids.com/nz/discover/animals/ sea-life/jellyfish-facts/
This website features a great round-up of facts about jellyfish, including their classification.

Invertebrates
www.ducksters.com/animals/invertebrates.php
To learn more about different kinds of invertebrates both on land and at sea, check out this website!

INDEX

bones 6, 22

carnivore 10

color 4

ecosystem 20

eggs 16

ephyra 16

humans 16, 18

invertebrate 6

life stages 14, 16

light 8, 10

medusa 14

nerve net 8

plankton 4, 10

poison 18

polyp 16

tentacle 10, 14, 18

touch 8